The Art of the Birdhouse

Flights of Fancy

by Mike Dillon

Photographs by Jim Cinna

Andrews and McMeel
A Universal Press Syndicate Company
Kansas City

The Art of the Birdhouse

ISBN: 0-8362-2704-2

Library of Congress Catalog Card Number: 96-86715

ATTENTION: SCHOOLS AND BUSINESSES
Andrews and McMeel books are available at
quantity discounts with bulk purchase for educational,
business, or sales promotional use.
For information, please write to:
Special Sales Department, Andrews and McMeel,
4520 Main Street, Kansas City, Missouri 64111.

Red Sky at Night

A Few Words from the Author

I started a company based on creative fabrication. As it has grown, I don't get to work with tools as often as I like. I began building birdhouses as a creative outlet, and I've used them for functional home decor as well as gifts. Birdhouses are a fantastic inspiration for using a variety of materials—once you abandon traditional rules of birdhouse construction, the sky's the limit.

This book is a collection of photos of some of the birdhouses that I've made. Photographed by Jim Linna, the birdhouses are shown in a variety of outdoor locations, as well as in the studio.

I've designed the book as an art book—as a gallery of beautiful images and intriguing designs. I hope you take as much pleasure in these flights of fancy as I have in creating them.

—Mike Dillon

for my wife Carol, and my sons, Zac and Oliver — *birds of a feather*

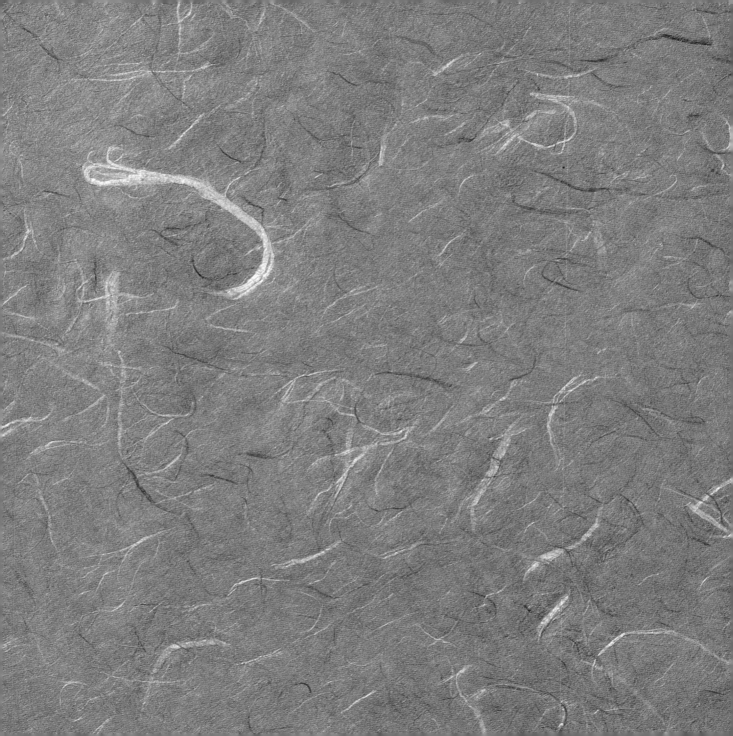

House of Twigs

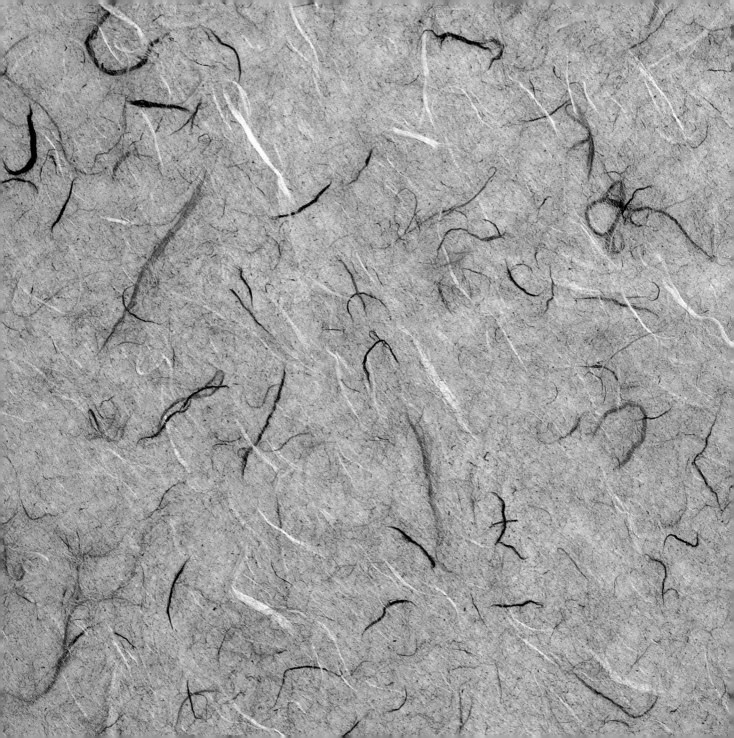

Bird Bath

Urban Flight

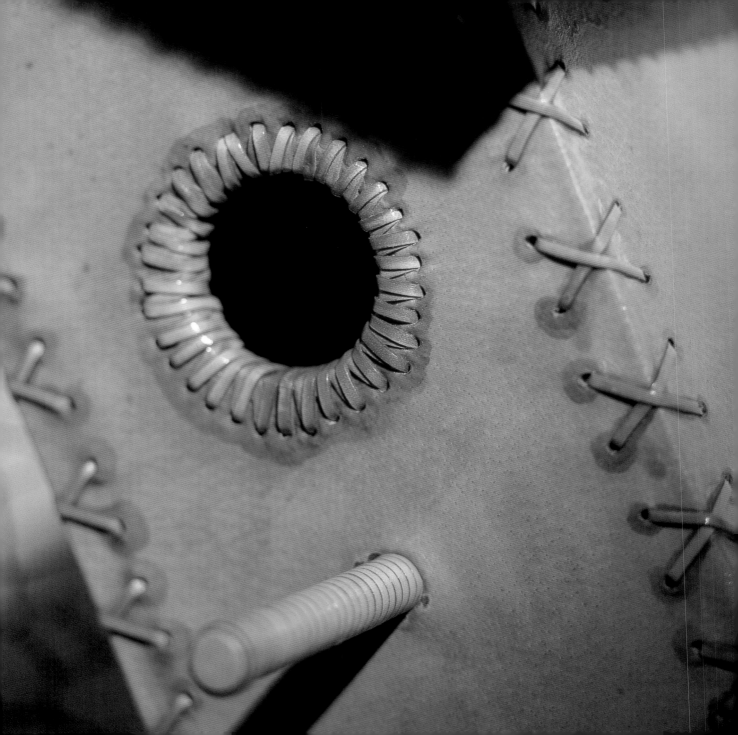

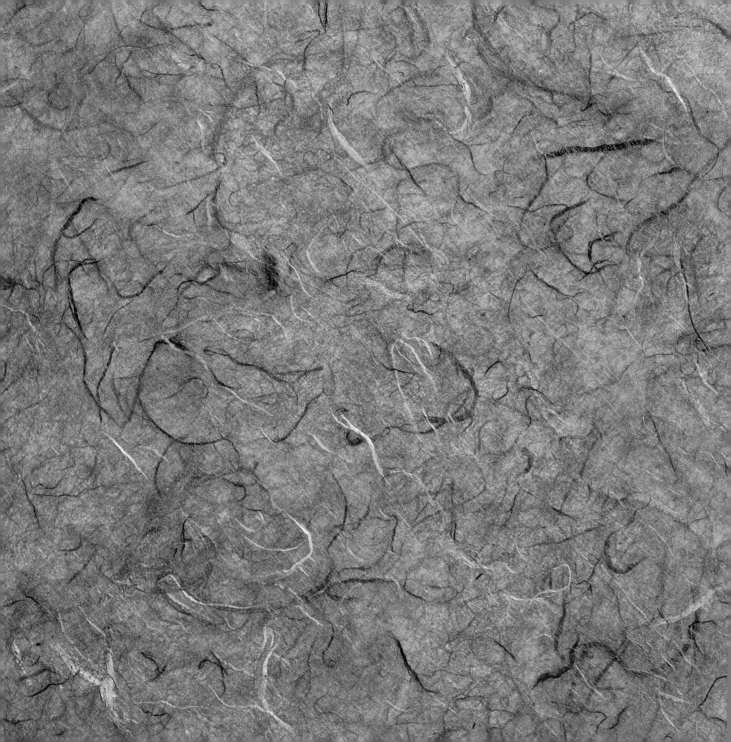

time Flies

Birds of a Feather

Weathered Friends

This Old Birdhouse

DarnWoodpeckers

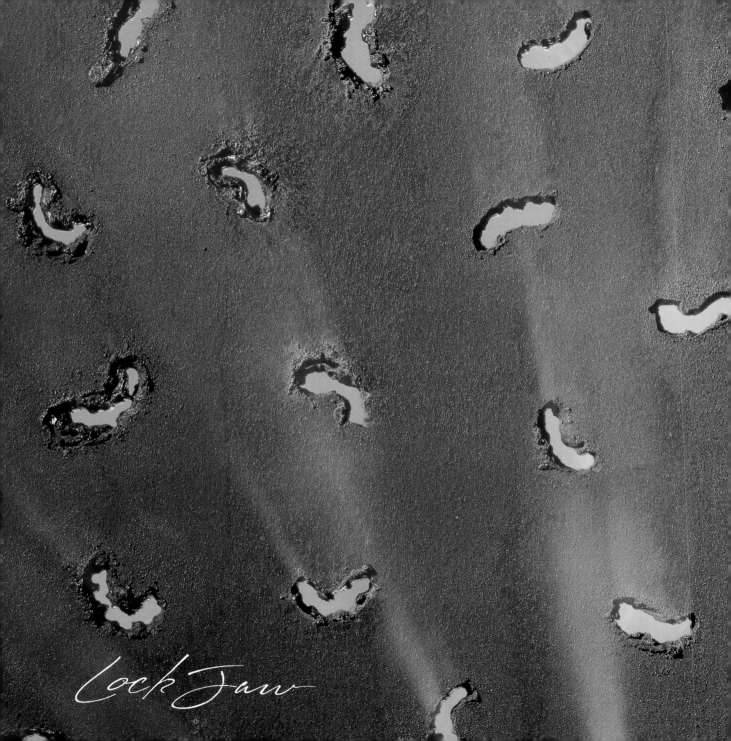

Pecking Order

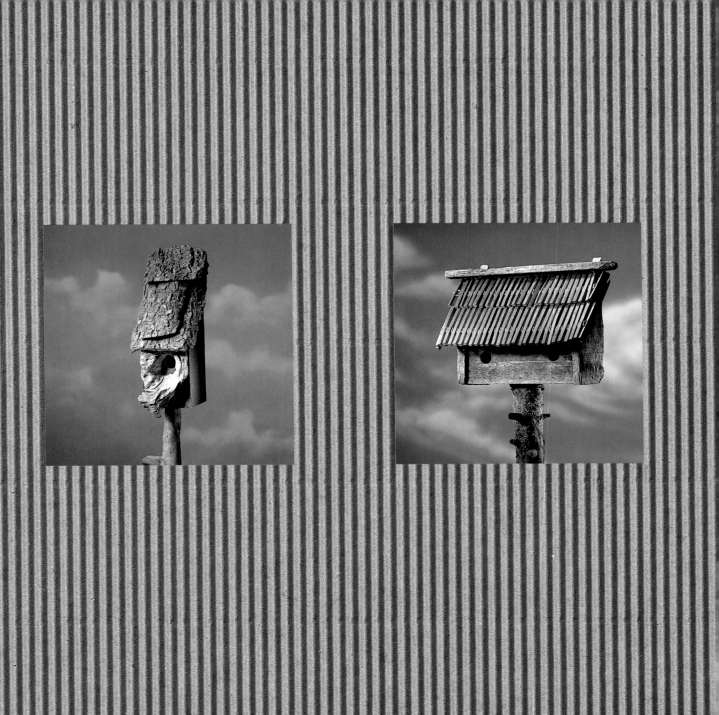

High Tea

A House in the Clouds

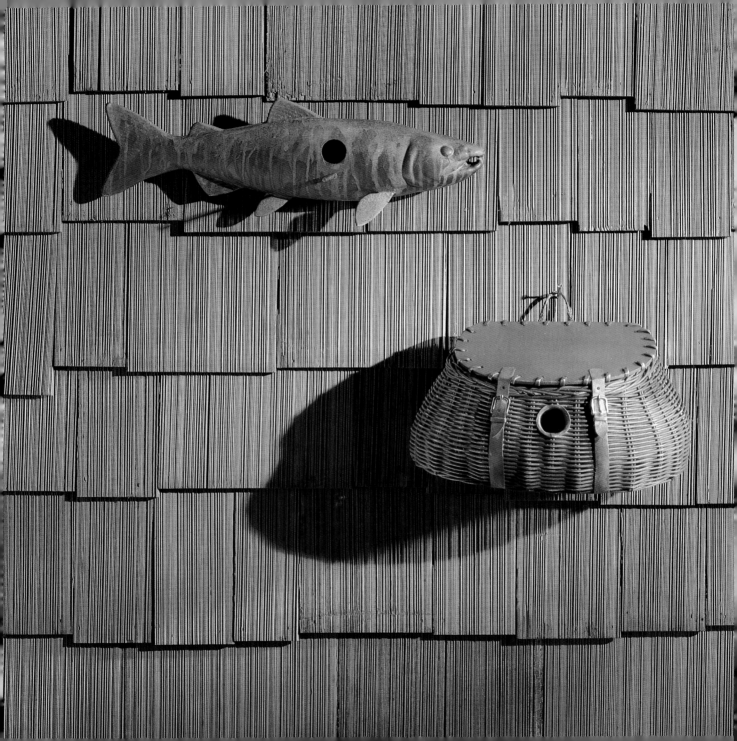

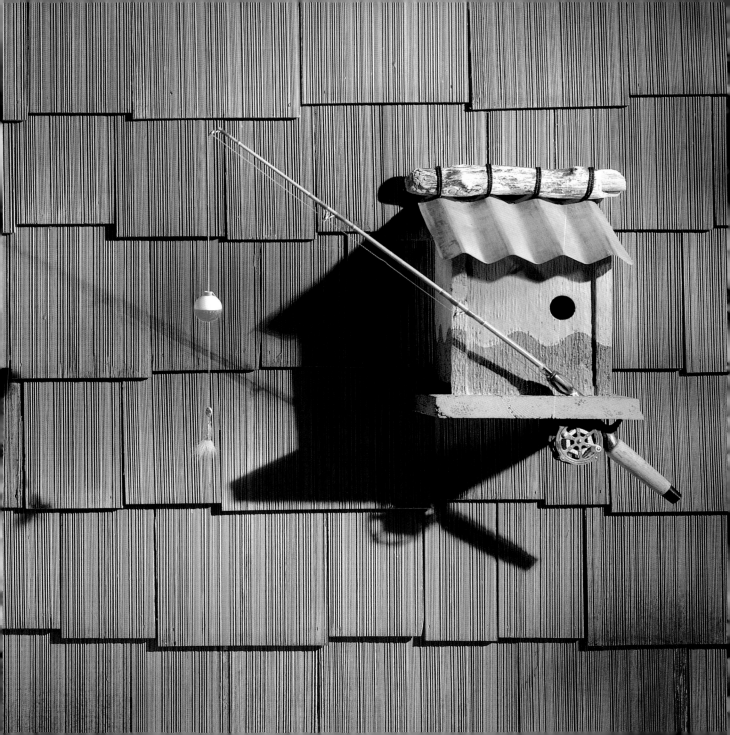

Eggtimer

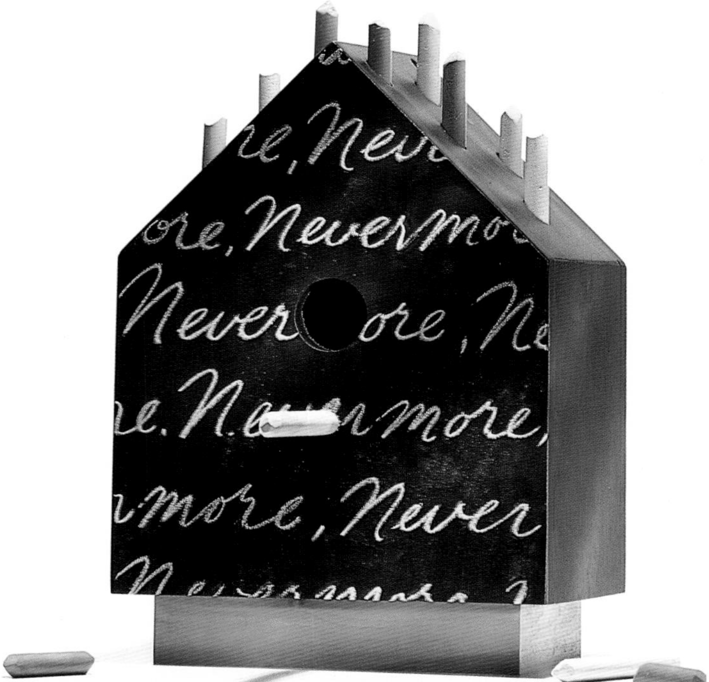
re, Neve
ore, Nevermo
Never ore, Ne
more,
more, Never

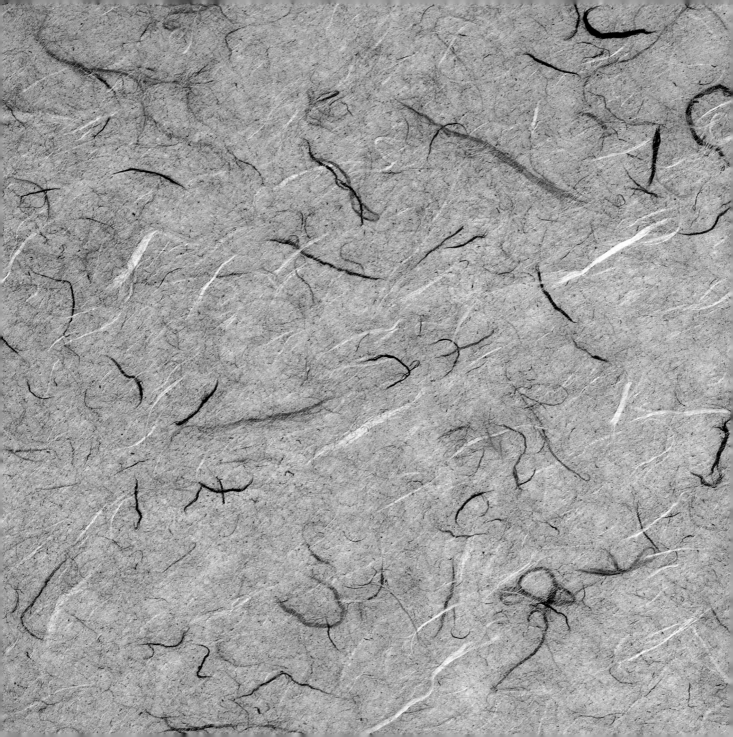